The Would You Rather Game Book For Kids

"A perfect gift for your young ones"

<u>Natalie Fleming</u>

Welcome!

Hi There,

This is my second book in the Kid Niche and I am very excited to share the content with you. You can check all my books by visiting the Author Profile.

As a token of appreciation I wish to share some Fun Slime Recipes with you.

Either Click <u>Here</u>

Or copy/type

http://eepurl.com/dtOspz

I would be sharing the new updates with you in coming months.

Cheers!

Natalie Fleming

Inside You Would Find

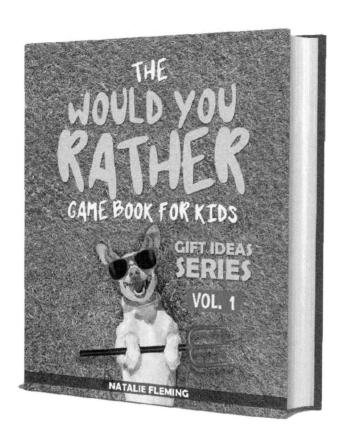

"In this entire world there is nothing as beautiful as a happy child."

L. Frank Baum

Hi There! I am Max. Let's go to through the interesting journey of "Would You Rather?" questions.

Hello Friend, I am Bella. If you like cats, I am sure you would come along with me on this fun ride!

Tip:

If you love Max: Ask his Questions!

If you like Bella: Ask her questions to your sibling, cousin or friend!

Would You Rather ?

Have a cat who barks or a dog that meows?

Go to past and meet your ancestors or future to meet your grandkids?

Would You Rather ?

Be trapped in a room with a friendly tiger or 20 bumblebees?

Be the funniest or the smartest kid in your class?

Would You Rather ?

Have 6 small gold fish or 2 large fighter fish in your aquarium?

Make a new toy or make a new cartoon movie?

Would You Rather ?

Introduce yourself by dancing or singing?

Ride a Boat or a Glider with your dad?

Would You Rather ?

> **Would you rather run like hippo or a giraffe?**

> **Have hot or cold weather throughout the year?**

Would You Rather ?

Be fast like an eagle or beautiful like a peacock?

Play with slime or dough?

Would You Rather ?

Go to space or deep sea?

Ride an elephant or a whale?

Would You Rather ?

Eat burgers or pizzas for the whole month?

Be sick for 5 days or get a shot from the doctor?

Would You Rather ?

Go to a sea beach or snow mountain for a week?

Choose a rose or a sunflower as your friend, if you woke up as a flower?

Would You Rather ?

Fly like a bird or swim like a fish for a week?

Play soccer or baseball in your school team?

Would You Rather ?

Have a playhouse or a trampoline as your Birthday gift?

Have a magic button to make your mom or dad stop talking for a day?

Would You Rather ?

Never have to take exam ever or never fall sick again?

Do a hokey pokey or the chicken dance?

Would You Rather ?

Live in a castle or a tree-house for a week?

Have a pet dolphin or a pet penguin in your pool?

Would You Rather ?

Own a real robot or rocket?

Meet a Unicorn or a Fairy?

Would You Rather ?

Have a truck load of doughnut or ice-cream?

Take powers of a magician or a super hero?

Would You Rather ?

Play hide & seek or snake & ladders?

Play outdoor game or watch indoor movie on a holiday?

Would You Rather ?

Like to be invisible or walk across the walls?

Be the president or a movie star for a day?

Would You Rather ?

Stay in a house boat or a RV for a week?

Have zero or one eyebrow for a day at your school?

Would You Rather ?

Know all animal languages or foreign languages?

Bring back wooly mammoth or a dinosaur from extinction?

Would You Rather ?

Have a unicorn Horn or Tail?

Have Fur or Scales on your body?

Would You Rather ?

Be Famous or Rich when you grow up?

Have more Time or Money?

Would You Rather ?

Lose the sense to smell or taste for a day?

Lose your hair or teeth when you grow old?

Would You Rather ?

Wear red or yellow costume (top to bottom) in your school party?

Plant a flower or a fruit in your balcony?

Would You Rather ?

Be a pilot or a scientist if a given an option?

Go to Disneyland or Lion Safari this summer?

Would You Rather ?

Fly to Mars or Moon on your rocket?

Count your hair or stars in the sky?

Would You Rather ?

Play a piano or a guitar in your annual day?

Play Ice Hockey in winters or Soccer in rainy season?

Would You Rather ?

Take a Tiger cub or a Lion cub to your neighborhood park?

Dance with a Chimpanzee or an Orangutan?

Would You Rather ?

Win an Olympic medal or Dollar Million lottery?

Race with Cheetah or swim with Shark?

Would You Rather ?

Fly to Africa or Australia on your private plane?

Go to Great Wall of China or Giza Pyramid with your family?

Would You Rather ?

Make a Triangular or Circular home?

Have a house made of Chocolate or Gummy Bears?

Would You Rather ?

Be a Fighter Pilot or a Fire Fighter?

Ride a Sub Marine or a Space Ship?

Would You Rather ?

Have powers to read mind or see future?

Live with Simbaa or Mowgli for a month?

Would You Rather ?

Make a new holiday or a new sport?

Pet a Koala Bear or a Panda?

Would You Rather ?

Swim in a river filled with Tomato Sauce or Egg Yolk?

Have an extra Finger or a Toe?

Would You Rather ?

Have Rabbit Tail or Tortoise Shell?

Live in a Forest or a Mountain for a week?

Would You Rather ?

Have pet Dragon or pet Jeanie?

Ride on back of a Hippo or an Elephant?

Would You Rather ?

Find a hidden treasure or win a lottery?

Eat the complete raw onion or lime?

Would You Rather ?

Camp in a forest or in hills?

Stay in underground hotel or space station for a week?

Would You Rather ?

Be Spiderman or Ironman for a day?

Go to a Dentist or a Doctor?

Would You Rather ?

Invent a new holiday or a new sport?

Have a pool or a tree house in your backyard?

Would You Rather ?

Wear a clown nose or wig for a day?

Become a Police Officer or a Detective?

Would You Rather ?

Invent a time machine or an invisible making machine?

Make a sand castle or chocolate fort?

Would You Rather ?

Drink water from a River or a waterfall?

Dress like a Clown or Aqua man this Halloween?

Would You Rather ?

Lose your Hearing or Vision for an hour?

Help in gardening or mow in the lawn?

Would You Rather ?

Read a story book or play board without electricity?

Grow fruits or vegetables in your terrace?

Would You Rather ?

Be stranded on an island or in a spaceship for a week?

Live with Mermaid in the sea or Fairies in the sky?

Would You Rather ?

Swim in river full of Chocolate or Ice Cream?

Wear summer dress in winter or warm jacket in summer?

Would You Rather ?

Jump like a Frog or hop like a Kangaroo?

Have Red hair or Yellow eyes?

Would You Rather ?

Quit Cell phone or T.V for a week?

Watch Rainbow or Lunar Eclipse?

Would You Rather ?

Have your dress or your shoes constantly change colors?

Have the power to read what Humans or Animals are thinking?

Would You Rather ?

Would you rather have second Birthday or Christmas in a Year?

Live for a week without running water or electricity?

Would You Rather ?

Walk on water or fly in air?

Read people mind or be invisible?

Would You Rather ?

Have a flying Carpet or a transparent submarine?

Go to Amazon Forest or Antarctica?

Would You Rather ?

Clean the table or wash the car?

Participate in school debate or sports?

Would You Rather ?

Do farming or rear cattle for a month?

Go fishing or camping with your friends?

Would You Rather ?

Visit Statue of Liberty or Eiffel Tower?

Write a sentence or a multiplication table?

Would You Rather ?

Ride an Ostrich or a Camel?

Live in a Cold or Hot Desert?

Would You Rather ?

Mix Black or Red color with White to get Grey?

Control your Anger or Laziness?

Would You Rather ?

Learn Boxing or Martial Arts for self defense?

Become Rabbit or Guinea Pig for a day?

Would You Rather ?

Have ear pierced or get a Tattoo?

Help with Grocery or do the Dishes?

Would You Rather ?

Make a rule or Break it?

Take help from someone known or anonymous?

Would You Rather ?

Do Math problem or babysit your sibling/cousin for a day?

Have Cookies or Doughnut every day?

Would You Rather ?

Choose Truth or Dare?

Find a hidden Treasure in the ocean or Aliens in the space?

Would You Rather ?

Spell Google or Amazon?

Order online or visit store?

Would You Rather ?

Drill to the other side of the earth or make ladder to the Moon?

Land on Jupiter or Mars?

Would You Rather ?

Watch Constellations or Shooting Star?

Eat on a Plastic plate or a Banana Leave?

Would You Rather ?

Learn Yoga or Taekwondo?

Keep small fish in a large or big fish in a small aquarium?

Would You Rather ?

Have a Parrot or a Pigeon as a pet?

Build a Bridge or a Dam?

Would You Rather ?

Eat Strawberry or Raspberry for an hour?

Live where it's always day or always night?

Would You Rather ?

Draw nature or face?

Wear under wear above your pant or socks over your shoes?

Would You Rather ?

Tie Shoe Lace or Tie for 100 people?

Have three Ears or Eyes?

Would You Rather ?

Have big moustache or pony tail?

Build Skyscraper or an Underground City?

Would You Rather ?

Do what interests you or what your friends are doing?

Talk or listen continuously for 6 hours?

Would You Rather ?

Have Robot or Jeanie as your friend?

Have 10 dollars now or 3 dollars per day for a week?

Would You Rather ?

Travel by Car or Train for a holiday?

Eat your favorite sweet before or after the meal?

Would You Rather ?

Talk over phone or meet the person?

Play in sand or snow?

Answer That ?

Pig who knows karate?

Bear cub without Teeth?

(*For Key refer page: 100-102)

Answer That?

Which Veggie has its own room?

Which softest creature to Fly?

Answer That?

Teacher's favorite Bee?

Why is Soccer Stadium cool?

Answer That?

A sleeping Bull is called?

It falls in winter but not gets hurt?

Answer That?

Which Tree I can hold in my hand?

What is Dad Corn called?

Answer That?

Where are Strawberry's parents stuck?

Which building in your city has most stories?

Answer That?

Which is the wealthiest plant?

What do volcanoes say before marriage?

Answer That?

Why did you bring ladder in the school?

Which is a vacation spot for Pencils?

Answer That?

Why Orange team lost the game?

Why does Zero wear a belt?

Answer That?

How does all the Birthday end?

I have hands but can't write?

Answer That?

Which race can't be run?

I have 2 legs but can't walk?

Answer That?

A subject taught at Snake Schools?

A Dog always likes Hot Summer Beach?

Answer That?

Which 5 letter word become smaller which we add 2 letters to it?

Which letter of the alphabet has most water?

Answer That?

Break me to use me?

I start with T, end with T and hold T?

Answer That?

Where Thursday comes before Tuesday?

You name me, you break me?

Answer That?

Can your pocket be empty and still have something?

I am a bank with no money?

Answer That?

You can't have these two for breakfast?

I am a cup which can't hold milk?

Answer That- Key

Pig who knows karate?	*Pork Chop*
Bear cub without Teeth?	*Gummy Bear*
Which Veggie has its own room?	*Mushroom*
Which softest creature to Fly?	*Butter Fly*
Teacher's favorite Bee?	*Spelling Bee*
Why is Soccer Stadium cool?	*It is full of Fans*
A sleeping Bull is called?	*Bull Dozer*
It falls in winter but not gets hurt?	*Snow*
Which Tree I can hold in my hand?	*Palm Tree*
What is Dad Corn called?	*Pop Corn*
Where are Strawberry's parents stuck?	*In a Jam*
Which building in your city has most stories?	*The Library*
Which is the wealthiest plant?	*Money Plant*
What do volcanoes say before marriage?	*I Lava You*

Why did you bring ladder in the school?	*Togo to High School*
Which is a vacation spot for Pencils?	*PEN-nsylvania*
Why Orange team lost the game?	*It ran out of juice*
Why zero wears a belt?	*To become 8*
How does all the Birthday end?	*With a Y*
I have hands but can't write?	*A Clock*
Which race can't be run?	*Swimming Race*
I have 2 legs but can't walk?	*Trouser/Pant*
A subject taught at Snake Schools?	*Hissss...tory!*
A Dog always likes Hot Summer Beach?	*Hot Dog*
Which 5 letter word become smaller which we add 2 letters to it?	*Smaller*
Which letter of the alphabet has most water?	*C*
Break me to use me?	*An Egg*
I start with T, end with T and hold T?	*Teapot*
Where Thursday comes before Tuesday?	*Dictionary*

You name me, you break me?	Silence
Can your pocket be empty and still have something?	Hole
I am a bank with no money?	River Bank
You can't have these two for breakfast?	Lunch and Dinner
I am a cup which can't hold milk?	Cupcake

Did the kids enjoy!

If yes, leave your kind comments and reviews. For suggestions reach out to us at <u>*Valueadd2life@gmail.com*</u>*.*

If you want to get Slime Making Recipes and receive updates about our new releases

Either Click <u>Here</u>

Or copy/type

http://eepurl.com/dtOspz

Cheers!

Natalie

Printed in Great
Britain
by Amazon